THE TOWN THAT NEVER WAS

A HISTORY OF 7A RESORT AND PIONEER TOWN, TEXAS

By

Patricia (Trish) Stanley Czichos

THE TOWN THAT NEVER WAS

A HISTORY OF 7A RESORT AND PIONEER TOWN, TEXAS

Patricia *(Trish)* Stanley Czichos

ISBN-13: 978-1534939622

Contents

Dedication

To the guests, employees, Wimberley residents,
and family members who lived them—

To Raymond L. and Raymond W. who photographed them—

To everyone who remembered and related them—

To the Czichos family—

Thanks for the memories!

And, as always, this is dedicated to the heart of my heart!

And to Chris and Wendy who made it fun!

Trish

Early Years

To tell the story of Pioneer Town, one must first tell the story of the family who created it. The year was 1946. World War II was over. Raymond Louis Czichos and his wife, Madge Wood Czichos, both Baylor graduates of the class of 1935, with their three children: Raymond Wood, Gene Francis, and Patricia Joanne; lived comfortably in Channelview, Texas, where R.L. had worked for Shell Oil as a chemist for ten years before and during the war. But Raymond and Madge had other plans. They decided that they wanted to raise their family in the country rather than in the booming industrial area near Houston, and, more than that, create a place where others could escape from the city. Madge's brother Carroll and his wife Lilah had a summer place in a small, relatively unknown town on the Blanco River--Wimberley. It seemed ideal for Raymond and Madge's dream.

After looking at numerous locations in the Hill Country from New Braunfels to Fredericksburg, the young family settled on 7.45 acres in Wimberley. With limited resources and much to the horror of their families, Raymond pulled his savings out of Shell's Provident fund and bought the land. It was about one mile off Wimberley's square and contained a gravel pit on the Blanco River. Deciding to call their new home Seven Acres Ranch, the Czichoses began a new chapter in their life.

Wimberley Square cir. 1940

Wimberley Square cir. 1940

Raymond L., and his father, Frank Czichos, built a workshop and small cabin for the family to live in during the summer of 1946. Then they built five stone cabins and a small recreation building above the river. Because there was no call for a chemist in Wimberley in 1946, R.L. leaned on his building skills and a hefty dose of confidence. He traded electrical and plumbing work with local rock masons to get his *"ranch"* up and going. Additional work to keep the family fed often was paid for in chickens or produce, which Madge's good cooking skills made full use of.

The summer of 1947 saw some of the Czichoses' friends from Channel-view come to spend time in the newly-opened resort. Slowly, through word of mouth in the Houston area, news spread of the comfortable vacation place on the Blanco, bringing more and more guests. R.L was a smart, hardwork-ing visionary. Madge was a creative and skillful artist and seamstress as

well as a good cook, and a caring, kind person who drew people to her. The children: 8, 6, and 1, were willing helpers. Soon the Czichoses had another son, Carroll Louis. Over the next few years, the Czichos family added a swimming pool and addi-tional cabins. Entertainment ranged from watching the Czichoses' home movies and hay rides in Wimberley

to fishing and boating on the Blanco River and swimming in the pool. Though operating on a shoestring, the business slowly grew. A pattern was set of building in the fall and winter, and entertaining guests during the warmer months. The six Czichoses were braced to create what more than sixty years later continues to operate as 7A Resort.

The Silver Spoon Cafe

Though all the cabins had cooking facilities, for those wishing to eat out or for larger groups like senior trips, the town of Wimberley had little to offer. So the idea of building a cafe on site took root. Early in the 1950's, in response to a demand for a large space to feed groups, the Czichos family decided to build a cafe. After pouring the foundation in the early fall of 1956 for a glass-fronted, modern restaurant, R.L. took his family to California to see the newly-developed Disneyland. While there, the family visited Knott's Berry Farm. The old western town spurred their imagination, and they returned to Texas to convert the soon-to-be built cafe into an Old West design. Because most of America was looking forward to the future, building with new materials like aluminum siding, R.L. soon found that Old West antiques and architectural pieces were readily available. In fact, most could be had for free or little expenditure. Old windows, doors, and columns were often pulled off burn piles or scrap heaps from places where modernization was occurring. For the effort of cleaning out sheds or barns, one could have whatever he found.

So the first building in what was to become Pioneertown (*early spelling*) was the Silver Spoon Café, which opened in 1957. Filled with twenty-two round antique oak tables, most bought for $2.50-$5.00 each on Red River Street in Austin, and a bar from the Metropole Hotel in Waco, Texas, which was already 110 years old,

the Silver Spoon was soon transformed into an *"old west"* venue. The back bar was rescued from a cotton field in Old Dime Box, Texas. The cedar mantel over the fireplace was a cedar log cut by *"Old Man Cowan."* The whole café cost about $6000.00 to build and furnish. The kitchen equipment came from Camp Gary in San Marcos, Texas. At one end of the café was a small General Store with a 1880 potbelly stove rescued from the Santa Fe Depot in Waco, Texas, and gift items. This area, which early on came to be more

financially lucrative than the café, eventually evolved into the Pioneer Emporium. To add to the western experience, entertainment was provided by local musicians, often in front of a roll-down canvas

backdrop hung in front of the fireplace. The Czichos daughters danced the can-can with their brother providing comic relief as another dancer.

Other times, guests would be taken on a hayride and fed outside. Later, as business increased, a dishwashing room and a smaller private dining room to accommodate larger crowds was added. By 1959, the Silver Spoon and 7A Ranch appeared in the Houston Chronicle's Rotogravure section.

Good Fortune

Active in the community where they found themselves, the Czichoses and their family business grew with the town. Still pulling most of its clientele from Houston and surrounding areas, Seven Acre Ranch was ready for expansion. With the completion of the Silver Spoon Cafe and cabins numbered 1-15 (*no 13 because it was bad luck!*), the original seven acres was filled.

Two events occurred to enable the Czichos family to expand even further. Madge Czichos received a small inheritance from a great aunt, and adjacent land became available for purchase. The seven acres suddenly doubled. With the acquisition of this land, a new direction could be explored. What had been the back of the property now could be used for further building. The additional acreage created enough space for a parking lot, but its location exposed the back service area of the cafe. To solve that problem, the Czichoses added *"fronts"* on two sides of the cafe building. On one side, a jail was built with bars and a cell from San Antonio. Next door to the jail, post office boxes from Stockdale became the main decorative piece for the

Pioneer Town Post Office. R.L. paid $1.00 per year to make it an official postal station with its own location stamped on each post card and letter mailed from there. Beside the Post Office was a barber shop complete with its own chair and personalized mugs for its customers.

Other buildings were represented by false fronts and display windows. Now visitors approaching the entrance to the Silver Spoon were treated to a glimpse of the Blue Chip Saloon, Wells Fargo office, Hotel, Pawn Shop, Barbershop, and Jail. A log stockade and fort was built to camouflage the workshop, originally created for construction purposes.

The Pioneer Emporium

During the first year of its operation, the Silver Spoon Cafe had been successful with the whole family taking part in the cooking, dishwashing, cleaning, and serving. But more successful had been the few gift items placed at the register for folks to purchase as they left. So the family decided to add to their town by building a gift shop, the large Emporium building. R.L. was once again scavenging for store displays and counters. Using many of the antiques which they had now accumulated, the Czichoses added on the Mercantile Museum, a nineteenth century general store. The imagination and talent of both Madge and Raymond were apparent everywhere as they artistically arranged displays and décor. The new building changed the orientation of the town. The Pioneer Emporium, in 1960 the second building to be built in Pioneer Town, was based on the Upjohn building on Disneyland's Main Street. Like Walt Disney, R.L. Czichos built Pioneer Town to a four-fifths scale. This practice made the town have a very cozy and human scale, but

presented problems when he found eight-foot doors from Victorian houses with twelve and fifteen foot ceilings. Often the doors and windows had to be adapted to the smaller scale. As many pieces of gingerbread and other Victorian trim and bricabrac were destined to be burned as buildings were modernized in the 1950's and early 1960's with aluminum siding, R.L. and his father were busy locating and retrieving such pieces to use in Pioneer Town. Many of the store fixtures in the Pioneer Emporium came from San Marcos Drugs, a business that had burned in 1922. The remaining cabinets dated back to 1905. The hanging light fixtures came from the old fort at Brackettville, Texas. The impressive wooden front doors came from Waco. For a time, in the portion known as the Mercantile Museum, an old telephone switchboard from the Nimitz Hotel in Fredericksburg, circa 1900, sat. It was the twin of one used in Wimberley when the family moved to town. At that time, there was an operator, Mrs. O.T. Egger, who worked out of her home on the Wimberley Square. *"Central"* connected everyone and knew everything. Comments like *"Oh, she won't answer because she has gone to visit her sister in San Antonio"* were common. The ornately carved 1910 wooden hearse, which still sits in this portion of the Emporium, came from Georgetown, where it had been stored in a barn for 35-40 years. After the owner's death, this elegant gray vehicle with its rubber tires for quietness was offered for sale by his children.

Entertainment

More and more visitors came. Friends like Spencer Guimarin, the pastor of the local Christian church, and P.H. Bowen, the school principal, came to help entertain guests musically with hayrides and singing in the cafe. Because these shows were popular, R.L., a bit of an entertainer himself, decided to add two new venues: an old time Opera House and the Wagon Camp for outside medicine shows.

Originally R.L bought wooden wagons to provide seating, which later gave way to benches. Boys from the YMCA camp across the river dressed up as Indians and sometimes attacked the guests seated in their semi-circle of wagons. Adding to the excitement were lighted arrows soaring down on wires until one almost set a cedar tree on fire!! During the 1960's, 70's, 80's, and even into the 1990's, the Medicine Show with most of its original cast provided hilarious evenings while Dr. U. Skinem sold his Cypress Creek Elixir.

In addition to the jokes and music of Spencer, the original Dr. U. Skinem, the cast included Mr. Bowen, Willie Higgs- a music teacher from San Marcos, R.L. Czichos, and his oldest son Raymond W. With various others joining them from time to time, these formed the nucleus of the Medicine Show remembered by generations of showgoers on Tuesday and Saturday nights throughout the summer months. Because at the core, these shows were put on by friends and family, it was not unusual to find family members like Mr. Bowen's son Bill or Willie's friend Wade Butler joining the group. Nobody had as much fun as the cast of the Medicine Show.

On Mondays and Fridays, guests at 7A could enjoy the Gay 90's Revue in the Opera House. There Willie Higgs again figured as the pianist and jokester with straight man, R.L. He also held down one-fourth of the Brass Rail Quartet, sometimes joined by his son Bill and cheered

on each week by his always present wife, Jacque. Each summer produced a new crop of young ladies to dance the can-can. Originally both Gene and Joanne Czichos were part of that group, later the granddaughters took their turns. Some years the Czichoses even boarded young ladies who wanted to perform in the shows and work at Pioneer Town. The magic of visiting Wimberley often produced a desire in teenagers to be a part of the fun to be had working or visiting 7A and Pioneer Town.

The Belle of the Brass Rail Saloon, a different young woman each year, sometimes provided experience in performing that led to the Miss Texas pageant for singers such as Sue Haney and Sally Moeller. Raymond Wood became famous for his Pecos Bill duet each night in which he spit out his teeth (*actually small navy beans*) into the front row of the Opera House crowd. The mini-melodrama, *"Little Nell,"* later spotlighted various grandchildren and son-in-law Dick Larson along with the regulars. A real melodrama was held each Thursday night by the Bijouberti Players and other theatrical groups. The tradition continued of making 7A and Pioneer Town a family affair.

The Opera House

A tornado in the late 1950's in Waco, R.L.'s hometown, damaged the third floor of a Masonic Hall located at 6th and Austin Streets. That floor contained an Opera House built in 1904. The Masons decided to do away with the damaged area. When R.L. heard about it, he hurried to Waco to negotiate for the purchase of a ready-made Opera House. Taking apart the building and making numerous trips from Waco to Wimberley with a flat-bed trailer, R.L. soon had all the parts to recreate the old opera house and just create a building around it. He had saved wall paneling, banisters, stairs, the wooden theater seats, the proscenium arch and brass rail which fronted the stage. Originally there were 485 theater seats, made of cast iron and bentwood connected in rows. One hundred and fifty were sold to a church. Two hundred were used, and the rest were burned in a field. The brass lights overhead came from the Travis Co. Courthouse, which was torn down in 1950. They dated from before 1900 . Austin, Texas, provided a 110 year old theater organ. The front doors of the Opera House came from a house at 12th and West Austin in Waco, as did the arched windows above. Local carpenter Tim Harris helped R.L. one whole winter to put together the building from the various parts. He copied the exterior design from Disney's Golden Horseshoe in California. Adding an 1890 front bar from a livery stable loft in Tomball, Texas, R.L. now had his Opera House.

Pioneer Town's Reputation Grows

During these busy years, more and more people heard of the unique little town in Wimberley. It appeared in the Houston Chronicle's Rotagravure

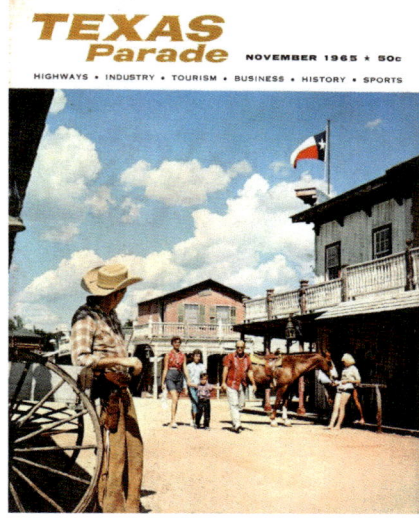

Section in 1959 and other newspapers and magazines. A western movie was filmed there, even though it was not a great one. The whole town was recognized by the American Museum Society. Pioneer Town was featured

on the television series The Eyes of Texas. Commercials, print ads, and music videos were ultimately filmed there. The resort was even endorsed by Duncan Hines.

The Bottle House

Having seen and heard about bottle houses which were built behind saloons in the old West to get rid of and use liquor bottles, R. L. became interested in having one of his own. Walter Knotts of Knotts Berry Farm had one built of champagne bottles. R.L. decided to make one of soft drink bottles. He was aided in this by Walter Feltner of San Marcos, who managed the Coca Cola bottling company there. Feltner generously opened his basement of old bottles to R.L., who promptly designed the bottle house which still stands in Pioneer Town today. With the help of local rock mason Bill Hamby, Raymond constructed the only bottle house in America made solely of soft drink bottles. Over 9600 bottles were used in its construction.

The Pioneer Gazette and Print Shop

Raymond L. continued to collect. He read everything he could find on the Old West and on antiques from the 1880's through the turn of the century. He wrote tirelessly to people that had old pieces for sale like printing presses and type for the new print shop. The Washington Hand Press from St. Louis was a real find, dating from the 1850's. The cast iron *"portable"* press, sometimes called a calendar or medicine counter press, was used by itinerate printers. The screw press was often used as an early copy machine for Western Union telegrams. The Zeitung Times of New Braunfels provided type and old papers as did the San Antonio Foundry for foundry type made with lead. The Pioneer Gazette gave R.L. an opportunity to print his own brochures and other marketing items like the Czichos family annual Christmas greeting and the newsletter which was to become the Pioneer

Gazette, a real newspaper telling of the doings at 7A each year.   For many years, the Print Shop created personalized wanted posters using old type. He even honored his father and mother by putting the years of their births, 1889 and 1887, over the doors of the Pioneer Gazette and the Blacksmith Shop.

The Ice Cream Parlor

R.L. always said that the Ice Cream Parlor built in 1963 was his favorite building in Pioneer Town. Having worked in a soda fountain during his youth when he had to carbonate drinks by using tanks of CO_2 and growing up in Waco, the home of Dr. Pepper, his favorite soft drink, he felt drawn to the idea of the old time Ice Cream Parlor. He reminisced about making Dr. Pepper milk shakes, Coke malts, ice cream sodas, and icing down the ice cream with salt and ice when he was a soda jerk in 1929. The coming of Hemisphere in 1968 in San Antonio provided the stone front and doors for the new Ice Cream Parlor when a home in central San Antonio was demolished. The Parlor's curving brass stair rail came from a San Antonio mortuary. The necessity of clearing out many of the old downtown buildings in San Antonio to make way for the big fair provided an additional treasure trove of building materials for Pioneer Town. The unique back bar was found in a barn in Smith Hardware in Stockdale, Texas.

The Arcade

Adjacent to the ice Cream Parlor was the Arcade building. Run by R.W. Czichos, it housed first a 100 foot slot car track. When that fad died, Raymond added pool tables, then ping pong and video games. For a time, the Corner Pocket store sold gifts and train tickets. Today it is still a place to gather and play for cabin and lodge guests as well as day visitors. Today called the Family Center Game Room, it not only has pool, ping pong, and vintage games but the Cowboy Corral for children's birthday parties.

Log Buildings

The Schlameus House

The building of Canyon Dam near New Braunfels from 1958-1966 gave new opportunities. Several old, small communities would soon find themselves at the bottom of Canyon Lake. R.L. salvaged three log buildings from that area, taking apart a cabin, outbuilding, and dog trot house, then numbering the logs to be reconstructed in Pioneer Town. The dog trot house located on the Eden Ranch in Satler, Texas, would later have the distinction of receiving the first Texas Historical Marker in this end of Hays County as the early home of the Schlameus family. Because it was 130 years old and already demolished when R.L. acquired it, this house proved the most challenging of the buildings in Pioneer Town to construct. For two years, R.L. says he just studied it. But when he finally discovered which logs were the base, it fit together *"like a puzzle."* He was able to fill it with numerous antiques found during his travels through Texas, including an armoire and rope string bed from the Maverick home in San Antonio, Texas. A very small log building came from the Krause family on the Jonas farm, which would be under Canyon Lake if it had not been rescued.

The Mill Building

The mill building was built as a replica of the original mill at Wimberley's Mill. The saw used was procured from Weldon Wimberley, from the basement of a building at Southwest Texas University used as a museum. It sat for many years under the overhang of the replica building until such time as Dorothy Kerbow, a descendant of Pleasant Wimberley, asked for its return. Of course, the Czichos family graciously returned it.

Family

During the late fifties and early sixties, the oldest Czichos son, Raymond Wood, went to Baylor, his parents' alma mater, to major in math education. His sister Gene soon followed, majoring in elementary education. Five years later sister Joanne attended Southwest Texas State College, majoring in elementary education also. Youngest brother Carroll continued at home with the three older siblings coming home to work at 7A during holidays. During this time period the three older children married and the first grandchild was born in 1965. The 1970's saw Carroll's marriage and five additional grandchildren. In the 1980's the last two grandchildren were born. During this time, Raymond Wood Czichos and his wife Trish moved to the ranch to live full time followed by sister Gene and her husband Dick Larson, then Joanne with her husband John White. Carroll with his wife Marie, *"Diddle,"* remained in Wimberley. All worked at 7A in various capacities.

Continuing Progress

But the growth of 7A Ranch Resort also continued. Over 100,000 guests had come to visit. The cabins numbered twenty. The Dodge House, a modern fourplex, was added near the Wagon Camp, and the four-room hotel style Pioneer House had been added on to the Opera House. An arcade, new post office, and bank extended Pioneer Town. A complete blacksmith shop was brought from Thrall, Texas. Carroll put in an indoor miniature golf course, which was soon moved outside and run by the grandchildren for a number of years.

The Lodges

In 1971 the first of three ten-room lodges was built, the Indian Lodge. Soon it was joined by the Cowboy Lodge, and later the Ponderosa Lodge. These large units with their spacious central meeting rooms and commercial kitchens catered especially to family reunions, church, school and business groups. During this time guests were treated to trail rides in the back part of the ranch, first through a concession held by David Lynn Domsch, whose grandmother and mother had helped cook at the Silver Spoon Café. Later Katy and Daniel Galpin ran the trail rides. Occasionally there was a shoot-out in the streets of Pioneer Town, again first with family and friends and later with more professional gunfighters from other Texas towns.

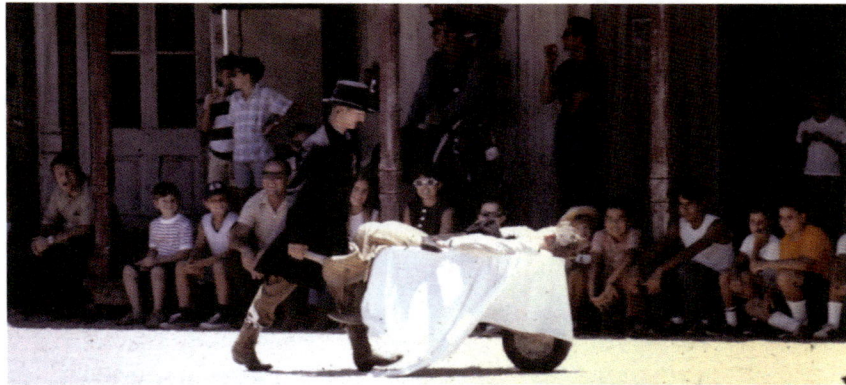

The Pioneer Town & Pacific Railroad

Also in 1971, A longtime dream of R.L. was fulfilled when son Raymond W. had a narrow gauge railroad built by Avey Bros. in San Marcos, Texas. Twins Roy and Ray Avey were park railroad enthusiasts, Roy having worked with Walt Disney in California in a live steamer hobby group. Beginning in 1971 the Pioneer Town and Pacific Railroad, with a half-scale replica of an 1870 wood-burning engine, a tinder, two passenger cars, and a caboose, took riders on a mile-long trip through the back acreage of the ranch. For thirty years, the drivers treated riders to a combination of corny humor and good fun, pointing out Mickey Mouse cactus and the Orr House, driving through the tunnel and emerging onto a trestle overlooking the distant hills and Old Iron Springs, *"the most re-lie-able springs around!"*

Pioneer Chapel

The last building to be built in Pioneer Town was the Pioneer Chapel. R.L., a devout Catholic, began collecting Spanish clay tiles for a mission style church. Madge, a devout Baptist, dreamed of a little white clapboard chapel. On a trip to Arkansas, the two saw a log chapel, which appealed to both, and so they compromised. Using a standard log cabin kit, the Pioneer Chapel was constructed. It became a truly ecumenical endeavor with its front doors from a Lutheran church on Zazamora Street in San Antonio, pews from St. Mary's church in San Antonio, painted glass windows from an Episcopal chapel in Waco, an upright piano from a Methodist church, and a pulpit from a Baptist church in Waco. The unique antique light fixtures inside the chapel are called gasoliers. Found in the basement of a department store in San Marcos in their original cartons, these were offered to the Czichos family to complete their church. Constructed at the beginning of the use of electricity, they were wired for such. But, just in case, they also contained reservoirs for oil or kerosene and a wick holder for backup lighting. Over the years, numerous weddings, quinceaneras, renewals of vows, and memorial services have been held in the Pioneer Chapel. It also served as the first home for St. Stephens Episcopal Church of Wimberley and the Wimberley Lutheran Church. It continues to be used on a regular basis.

Western Art

During the 1980's R.L. Czichos became a western art print dealer, buying and selling the artists that he so admired. During that time, he acquired a particular fondness for Frederick Remington, both his two-dimensional art and his bronzes. R.L began buying bronzes at that time. Soon he had amassed most of those done by Remington and determined to obtain one of all of them. As soon as he had them, he began to look for a place to display them. Although his first plan was to donate them to the Wimberley Library, on whose board he served, in a gallery to be built, that enterprise did not come to fruition. Not to be deterred, he then decided to build his own gallery, which is now known as the Pioneer Museum or, more familiarly, as the Remington Museum. Hidden in a grove of trees, it sits adjacent to Pioneer Town and contains in addition to the Remington bronzes, a collection of bronzes by New Mexico artist J.D. Woods and another by Charles Russell. Assorted other works round out the collection, as well as a silver commemorative statue of Remington's Bronco Buster and a display of Russell and Remington commemorative coins.

The Eighties and Nineties

The 1980's and 90's saw many changes come to the resort. The eight grandchildren were growing up and leaving for college-over half to their grandparents' alma mater, Baylor University. The family lost their beloved *"DeDe,"* Madge Czichos, in 1994. The men who had performed in the shows for over thirty years were growing older. New faces appeared, and the shows changed with them. As time passed, attendance dropped so much that they were no longer part of the summer routine. Now the only place to see the Medicine Show and Gay Nineties Review is the video put together by the family and available for purchase in Pioneer Town. But guests still came, many in their third generation of spending time at 7A and Pioneer Town and relaxing in the cool waters of the Blanco River.

A New Century

The twenty-first century saw a new focus at 7A Resort. The Silver Spoon Café was no longer open in the summers for the public, but became a venue for parties, receptions, and meetings. The fixed chairs in the Opera House were removed to give more flexibility for parties, allowing receptions and dances requiring an open floor. Weddings began to be held there. Smaller weddings took place at the Pioneer Chapel with receptions after in the Opera

House or Silver Spoon. Larger celebrations took over Pioneer Town completely when they took to the streets for large crowd events. Local charity My Neighbor's Keeper began its annual Mardi Gras celebration there. The Pioneer Emporium was rented

by well-known *"Texas"* Jack Glover to house his Cowboy Museum. Family reunions came year after year to the lodges, which suited their needs perfectly.

They could swim in the river and let their children roam through Pioneer Town while the older folks sat comfortably in the lodges. Each year a new group of high school and college students worked in Pioneer Town

and made their own memories while serving the guests. The family lost R.L. Czichos, *"Papa C,"* in 2003, and reorganized the business to suit all of the family members. And the guests still continued to come, finding in the

rustic cabins on the banks of the Blanco River a quiet reprieve from their busy lives. The town of Wimberley became a tourist mecca, giving the visitors even more opportunities to shop and eat out downtown than ever before.

Wimberley Goes Hollywood

In 2012, a film company approached Pioneer Town to film a movie for television, *Deliverance Creek*. This was by far the biggest enterprise to use Pioneer Town as one of its sets. Large parts of the town were modified to accommodate the Civil War story, and some of those changes were incorporated to change the face of Pioneer Town more than all the changes which had gone before. Throughout its history, various buildings like the Post Office have moved from one place in town to another. Other buildings have had their uses and facades changed. The First National Bank became Calico Craft shop after the bank furnishings were sold to the Sundowner Bank in Houston. The Craft shop later became the Frontier Rose, then the Sheriff's office, which had originally been near the Silver Spoon Café entrance. The Post Office was moved with the coming of the movie company and in its place, Madge's Millinery and Dressmaking Shop was created to honor Mrs. Czichos, who was a wonderful seamstress. Papa C's Gifts honored Mr. Czichos. The Pioneer House became Meg's Boarding House. New porches were added and boardwalks. Like all towns, Pioneer Town changed with the times.

Memorial Day 2015

Throughout the years, the Blanco River often rose with the spring rains to flood its banks and sometimes even the River Road. It had a few times reached the level of the swimming pool above its course, but it had never threatened even one of the cabins. Longtime guests were used to such events and often watched the river rise from their porches, even in mid-summer. But Saturday of Memorial Day in 2015 proved to be an entirely different event.

Following a long drought, the weather of the late spring was rainy, saturating the ground at 7A. But more than that, the headwaters of the Blanco and various other tributaries coming into it coupled with a severely heavy rain in Blanco , Texas, and sent thousands of gallons of water downstream. Every cabin and lodge was full, but the Czichos family was warned and able to evacuate all guests who were in possible danger. Sunday morning revealed the extent of the devastation. Fifteen cabins were gone or damaged beyond repair. The Dodge House had water in its lower level. The mighty cypress trees which framed the Blanco were stripped of their bark or ripped out by their

roots. Lives were lost, and homes destroyed. Life along the Blanco River would not be the same for many years. Like others devastated by the flood, 7A Resort faced hard times ahead. Mercifully, historic Pioneer Town was not touched, nor was the office or three lodges. Within hours, friends, guests, strangers, and family began the clean-up. *"Wimberley Strong"* became the cry of the day. 7A was able to continue the summer season on a limited basis with families returning to the lodges, guests to the remaining units, and events in Pioneer Town-one wedding one week after the devastation!

Then unbelievably, Halloween of 2015 brought another flood, this time more from run-off and doing more damage in downtown Wimberley along Cypress Creek. However, the Cowboy Lodge and many parts of Pioneer Town found themselves underwater. What a year!

Serendipity

So many things happened to create the magic of 7A and Pioneer Town that took root in the hearts of thousands of people. The Czichos family started their great adventure at a time when Americans were looking forward to a new prosperity that would enable them to take vacations, a time when a war-weary nation could cherish family and fun again. It also occurred when many pieces of architectural ornamentation and structures became readily available due to modernization. The coming of Hemisphere 68 in San Antonio, the building of I 35 through old parts of Austin and Waco, and the creation of Canyon Dam and Lake all made available parts of buildings that were going to be destroyed. It came at a time when people were fascinated by the Old West and wanted to be a part of it. It came at a time when people were willing to let go and laugh at simple, corny humor. But a story told by Mr. Czichos in his eighties shows how easily it could never have happened. In 1956 he took his family in a 14 foot Mobile Scout trailer to California to see Disneyland, but he miscalculated how much gas pulling the trailer would take, six miles to the gallon. In Ozona, Texas, he realized that he would not have enough money to buy gas to get to California. The year before a friend who owned a gas station had given him a Sinclair paper credit card, and he had put it in his wallet. Never having used anything like it, he decided to try so he wouldn't have to tell his family they were going home. That lucky card enabled the family to see Knott's Berry Farm and Disneyland, which was the inspiration for Pioneer Town, the town that almost wasn't—except for an early credit card. So whatever happens in the future of Pioneer Town, one can only hope that its luck will hold and those seven acres on the Blanco River will continue to be special to generations to come.

Afterword

After the disastrous two floods of 2015 and other family considerations, the Czichos family decided to sell 7A Resort to the Scott Way Group. The Way family has deep roots in Wimberley, maintaining a summer home just down the road from 7A. The Czichoses know that Scott will bring a new chapter in the history of 7A, one yet to be written, and hope that he will meet with all the success and joy that this little portion of the Blanco River has given them.

Raymond and Trish

Dick and Gene

Joanne and Johnny

Carroll and Diddle

And all the Czichos grandchildren and great grandchildren

Darrell, Chris, Kelly, Jon Ann, Wendy, Jason, Jacy, and Cari

Presley, Madison, Parks, Kendall, Landry,
Mason, Carson, Caylin, Taylor

Made in the USA
Charleston, SC
27 August 2016